King of the Sunset Strip Volume Three: The Poetry Collection.

By John Davies.

COPYRIGHT JOHN DAVIES 2018 ©.

All rights reserved. No parts of this publication may be reproduced or transmitted by in any form or by any means without permission of the author of the individual work.

Books by John Davies:

- King of the Sunset Strip Volume One: The Poetry Collection.
- King of the Sunset Strip Volume Two: The Poetry Collection.
- Black Paradise Society: Poems from an Insane Mind.
- Stood up by The Devil: The Poetry Collection.
- King of the Sunset Strip Volume Three: The Poetry Collection.

"Dedicated to Cooper & Carter Davies, and the eternal memories of Clint, Wayne & Spencer Davies".

John Davies 2018 ©.

You asked me to dissect myself
To see what I found inside.
If anything. All I saw was a
Darkness. An inky black hole
Where once was a heart.
The arteries pumped an oily
Liquid that I assumed
Was once blood but was
Forever changed along the
Journey through life.
The future once called
My name but all I can
Now see is a past that
Echoes ghost voices in
My mind. It is the call of
The lost trying to find
Their way home again
But getting lost along the way.
Getting stuck in the vortex.
Alone and forgotten souls.
We made them this way.

John Davies 2018 ©

You detected a heartbeat so assumed
I was alive. I was actually in mourning
And didn't want to speak to
Anyone. This had been a tough
Year and one I wanted to
Forget, yet all you ever did
Was remind me of everything
I was walking away from.

John Davies 2018 ©

Her smile was infectious
And I melted under
The heat of her gaze.
She had lips that I
Wanted to kiss
But her mind was
Like a maze.

John Davies 2018 ©

Three words I always
Wanted to say to you
And not the ones
That you wanted to hear.
You thought they were
I Love You
But I chose to say
Goodbye for Now.
Then walked away.

John Davies 2018 ©

Sometimes I wonder
How it will all end
And then realise that
It doesn't really matter.
I've set my stall up
In the latter years of my life
To take things daily.
To not set goals anymore
As they always seem to get in the way.
I want to spend every
Moment with the ones I love.
Everything else is a bonus.

John Davies 2018 ©

You flew past me
And settled on
A nearby Acer tree.
The most delicate
Butterfly I had ever seen.
I went to take a
Photograph of you
But you flew away
Into wherever you were
Going next. I wonder if
That is what happens to
Our spirits once it's
Our time to go.
Do we just float away?
Into the ether?

John Davies 2018 ©

We used words
Instead of wisdom
And wondered why
It always had the reverse
Effect. We chose anger
Over patience and when
The sirens sounded
It was you & I who ended
Up in the back of the
Meat wagon with a cold
Night ahead of ourselves
In a cold cell and the silence
Of the world around us.
I awoke sober, and felt stupid
As the walk of shame approached.
I watched them argue from across the sidewalk
And it immediately struck me how funny
People really are once they have lost control
Of their selves and their faculties. No shame.
No self-respect. They launched
At one another like wild animals and for a
moment they had forgotten that
At some stage in their lives
They had actually loved
One another. The poison inside
Now eating away at everything
They once held sacred.
This is the fall out of a very bad relationship.

John Davies 2018 ©

I found solace in our Friendship.
You could always chase the demons
Away from me. In that time
Together I felt safe. You were
My comfort blanket and
I knew I was untouchable.
I sipped Moet et Chandon
Ate cold salmon in the garden
And listened to Venus in Furs
By the Velvet Underground.
The birds sang along and it made me
Think about how the summers were
In Los Angeles in the 1960's
When all the heavyweight
Rock stars were still around.
I wondered how it would have
Felt to sleep on the beach
Under the stars and submerge
Myself in to that world.
Or the summer of love in
San Francisco. I wanted to spend
My whole life as a Poet.
Writing always and reaching out
To as many people as possible.
I wanted people to read my books.
To purchase and feel the book
In their hands. To submerge
Their selves into my world.

John Davies 2018 ©

A magic circle of friends
Was always going to be enough
It wasn't about being greedy.
I had you, therefore
I didn't need anymore
Then I already had.
For once in my life
I finally felt complete.

John Davies 2018 ©

We ate Chinese takeaways
Drank Thunderbirds & cheap cider.
Played spin the bottle, sat on park benches
Listening to The Shamen,
Oasis and The Happy Mondays
And plotted how we were
Going to skip school the next morning.
We were the generation terrorists of the 1990's
And we were about to be unleashed
Into the real world. We thought we knew it all.
Spent every night spending
Our minimum wages at the
Local pubs at a time where
A mouthful of someone else's
Cigarette smoke smacked
You in the face as they exhaled
That shit upon you. Trudging home with just
Enough bus fare to your dead end job first thing
In the morning. We made up
The rules as we went along
But these were the years that defined the adults
We eventually became.
And I'd never change those years for anything.
Years for anything for the
Knowledge and experience' I took with me
Made it possible to live my dreams
And do what I loved best.
Park life college at its finest.

John Davies 2018 ©

The landscape
Around us dissolved
Into dust. We sat with
Sores on our feet
And broken smiles.
It was meant to get
Easier the older we became.
Instead we found our
Future bleak and empty
Of any promise.
The town drunk stumbled
Into view and exited
Stage right. Wandering off
Into the sunset without
A care in the world.
Somehow, he had
The right idea.

John Davies 2018 ©

I was the younger brother
In a very disfunction family.
I was lucky enough to
Enjoy the 90's and the pub
Culture. Going home with
Smoke smell and lipstick
Face without ever getting the
Hard on to the next level.
I felt cheated. I was young.
Stupid. I felt that I held the
Knowledge of the universe
In the palm of my hands.
I fell asleep listening to
The Red Hot Chili Peppers
Under the Bridge. Los Angeles.
These are my kind of guys.
The Doors, Hendrix, Bowie.
Became obsessed with them all.
I swam in their music
And words and learnt
My art from the very best.
It gave me a platform
To work upon going forward.

John Davies 2018 ©

I can sit in the
Garden alone
At midnight
And feel content.
I didn't need this
World anymore
Or the strangulation
Everyday gives us.
Like an unwanted
Christmas present
We can hand it back
In a moment.
We can gain release
Finally.

John Davies 2018 ©

I have an Angel
That looks over me.
I call her Destiny.
She is a Mermaid.
I found her in my
Youth when I was lost.
I took too many pills
To numb my pain
And as I drown
I felt her pull at
My ankles and bring
Me back ashore.
She gave me the kiss
Of life and then
Left me alone.
I knew why she had to leave.
I just wish that
She could have taken
Me with her. I fell in love
Yet my heart remained
Broken.

John Davies 2018 ©

It's 22:15pm and alone
I sit at my garden table.
Pitch dark except a candle,
A glass of cold wine
And the sounds of my
Next door neighbours
Fish pond. Overhead the
Sound of an aeroplane
And late-night traffic.
The sky is a deathly blue,
Almost a cloudy violet.
The mosquitos avoid the
Flame on my table but
The sound of the foxes
Pierce the night.
I adorn four days stubble
On my face and await a
4am wakeup call but
The tequila still pours
And I just cannot get
Enough of this moment
Together.

John Davies 2018 ©

Still not fazed by it all.
The silence comforts me.
I fall asleep in the arms
Of Mother Nature like a
Child in the arms of a parent.
It's moments like this
I will miss once I'm gone.

John Davies 2018 ©

Awoken by the sounds
Of modern-day suburbia
On my one day off.
8am and the madmen
Are killing my dreams
And tearing up the road
Outside my bedroom window.
The morning sun already
On the rise. I long to be baked
By its glare once I wander
Outside into whatever chaos
Awaits me. I will fall foul to
Others bad decisions and return
Home frustrated by the stupidity
Of it all. At night I will sit down
And watch the sunset with a
Cold bottle of San Miquel.
I will evaluate my day
And every detail of it.

John Davies 2018 ©

The experiences we have
In life not only define our
Characters but also adds
To the teachings we will
One day share with our
Own children. If we allow any
Negativity to flow freely
From inside of us it will spread
And those around us will be
Affected by it like a common cold.
We have no cure for this
Particular illness and all that
It does is drag others into
The abyss with us.
It doesn't enrich their lives.
It infects and poisons therefore
It is better to emit the light always.

John Davies 2018 ©

You were my safety valve.
My comfort zone.
The blanket I wrapped myself
Up in. Like most things
In our lives I took you for
Granted. That I would have you
In my life forever. But time
Has no respect. We run through
Life like the sand in an egg timer.
We sift through darkness and
Try to come out on the other side.
We look at old photographs
And try to remember old times
When life was simpler.
We didn't have that responsibility
That was forced upon us as adults.
We felt cheated. Forever lost.

John Davies 2018 ©

The blank stare.
That dead look in your eyes
Told me everything I needed
To know. I thought you were
A fighter but you were
Prepared to back down
And let this addiction win.
We don't choose to fight
Temptation as it whispers
In our ear like a vixen.
It jumps on us and wrestles
Us to the ground.
Waiting for us to tap out.
Every morning you say today
Will be the game changer
And by the time evenings
Come around you're back
On the losing team.
Tomorrow you will say
The same thing and with
The same result until one day
You will not awaken
And the game will be over.

John Davies 2018 ©

I say to myself that
Today will be very
Different from yesterday
And that tomorrow I
Will culminate those
Learnings. Yet I find
Myself once more
Doing the same things
I had promised myself
That I would stop doing
In order to regain
Control and some sort
Of balance in my life again.
Work. Eat. Drink. Repeat.
A small amount of sleep
Along the way makes
This a tiring journey
For the body and my
Machine is full of flaws
And I look in the mirror
At myself and I wonder
How many miles I have
Left on the clock.

John Davies 2018 ©

Walking down the Sunset Strip.
Midday. The bars were full
It was a weekend. People drinking
And being over loud. The sidewalks
Were full of teen spirit and lipstick.
The was a fire in a remote part
Of town. No one attended.
We had a new Sheriff onboard.
He wore a white shirt and a big hat.
A swagger that made his hips
Look like a pole dancer
In a cheap late-night bar.
His name was Hope. He had none.
We walked past him like
The two devils from the apocalypse.
Boot heels scuffing the floor
And leaving dust in our wake.
His eyes gave the game away.
He knew we were the real
Generals in this town.

John Davies 2018 ©

Blood moon
Blood orange
The sweetest fruit
I ever savoured.
We turn full circle
Symmetrical balance
And the universe
Revolves on its
Axis once more.

John Davies 2018 ©

Surround yourself
With amazing people
That reflect only
The beauty that you
Have within yourself.
It is easier to have a demon
That whispers in each ear
Distracting you from
Getting on with your life
But the idea is to eject
All forms of darkness
And stay with the confines
Of everything that brings
You happiness and leaves
You with a smile on your face
Everyday. This time is ours
And our time is now.
Do something amazing today!

John Davies 2018 ©

Sometimes I think about
The future and it makes
Me smile. I look around
And realise that I have
Assembled the most
Amazing people in the
World to share my life with
And it makes me proud.
The memories we still have
To enjoy together. The fun that
Time gives us to achieve
Everything we have planned.
I sit alone late at night
And wonder who would ever
Want a night alone talking
About life while watching
Cocoon and drinking wine
With a really great pizza.
Think its time to start
A group chat with a cast
Of strangers and learn
More about others. This is the
Beauty of social media.
We can WhatsApp and never judge
One another. Life's an experiment.
Who wants to play?

John Davies 2018 ©

I feel ashamed of myself for
Complaining that I didn't have enough
Time for a proper drink and breakfast
This morning while there
Are people and young children
Dying of severe water shortages
And starvation in other pars
Of the world. Burning under a
Blazing sun that seeps what
Little energy they have from them.
I complained that the clean bath
Water was too cold because of the hot
Water outside. A rare heatwave I wasn't
Prepared for. I complained as I sat in a
New car with air conditioning while they walked
On red hot soil with blistered,
Cracked feet. I complained as I
Walked into my job that paid me
The money to keep my own family
Spoilt. One day I will complain
That I never had the humility
That others do who had nothing
And this makes me sad. Sometimes we just need
To be grateful for everything that we do and don't
have and think of those who have nothing, but
never complain about the fact they don't.

John Davies 2018 ©

I sit here
And watch the
Rain fight for
My attention
And still I have
Never heard your voice.
We drift through life
With no sense of direction
And wonder why we
End up at a dead end.
Confused and in a state
Of panic. There are
No footprints to lead us
Back to where we came from.
The world came apart
And you were no longer
With me.

John Davies 2018 ©

You saw me at
My worst. I was a
Hangover short of
A broken mind.
Role reversal. You were
No longer my boss.
I sat here watching
Kids TV on the big screen
And realized exactly
What I'd compromised
In becoming your adult.
It wasn't my intention
To play your glove puppet.
You held out your hand
I wiped out your smile.

John Davies 2018 ©

You bring out the worst in me and
Somehow always make me feel like
I am never good enough.
It was time to move on.
I felt abandoned & thrown away
Like an unwanted Christmas present.
I looked down at my feet
And two plastic bags
Resembled my lifetime
Achievements in a snapshot.
This was to be the foundations
Of how I moved forward.
I stayed on a friend's couch
And drank Campbells soup
While writing poems about
Andy Warhol's Pop Art
And a factory covered from
Head to toe in tin foil.
I fell asleep each night
Bemoaning the material
Objects that I once owned
While secretly laughing
At the sham of a life I had left behind.
In that instant, I became liberated again.
The future looked much clearer.
The elixir of life was held up high
Above my head for all to see.
Yet a sip never passed my lips.

John Davies 2018 ©

I felt sorry for him.
We stood graveside
And listened to the
Poorly chosen music
By a family who really
Had no finger on the pulse
Of the body that was
No longer alive.
He was a playboy.
A show off. He drove
A fast car. Spent weekends
In Monaco with five & dime
Whores. The King of a bankrupt
Empire. The credit card hero.
In life, he was a paper God.
In death he was the debt
That he left behind for others
To clear in his absence.

John Davies 2018 ©

Alien eyes. My Telekon.
Future love paradise.
You drank from the font
Of life and peeled away
My layers. Darby Crash &
The Germs screamed away
My peace in the background.
Minor success. Punk scene.
Late 70's. more cult through
The suicide clan than talent.
We worship tragic heroes.
There's a town called
Nowheresville.
Apparently, the ghost
Of Jim Morrison is opening
The show for a guy
Called Elvis. He was due
On stage in about 10 minutes.
I'd better check the burger
Van queue. He ordered five
Burgers and fries before heading
Off to the shitter and all
We needed was a performance
And not another dead rock star.

John Davies 2018 ©

I rolled out off the bed
And the sound of the
Garbage trucks and smell
Of the old lady next door
Giving her early morning
Cigarette the world's best
Blow job and swallow act
Was enough to inspire me
To shower and walk down to
The cheap seats and watch
Vito make the best eggs
In the world. I drank burnt
Coffee that was bitter
And hurt my throat.
I sat in the shade
And waited until my order
Had arrived.
White pepper made my eyes
Sneeze. My eyes were red
From last night's party.
I was due to be the local
Talent with his story
On a cheap radio show.
I drove out with an ice cream
In my hand and a surfboard.
The girls out back were twins.
I was not going alone.

John Davies 2018 ©

We were all a part
Of a broken machine
And no matter how hard
We tried, the winning streak
Was over and the awards
Stopped coming our way.
Always used to being
Number one, a place we
Took for granted.
Our leader departed
And the game ended.
Leaving us with egg
On our faces and bruised
Egos. Some will raise
Their game once more
While others will depart
Or become casualties.

John Davies 2018 ©

Be careful what you read
And buy into.
Pick up a book and
Ignore bad poets like
Myself. Don't seek the
Answers from an hourglass.
There is a war raging
And everyone's a critic.
In the background
Is a ghost and he is
Always watching you.

John Davies 2018 ©

People ask me why
I never smile.
I am ugly. I don't have
Smiley teeth and
Someone that will
Iron the lines from my
Face. The grey is showing
In my hair and not receding
Yet but the signs are
Hanging over my demise.
And I'm happy to
Acknowledge the fact
Now that I've become
Old and irrelevant.
I try to dress well
To cover over the cracks
Like we do with wallpaper
In a derelict house.

John Davies 2018 ©

I woke up too early
This Sunday morning.
Made coffee and put
A chicken in the oven.
Was meant to hit 80
Degrees by midday
And off to visit my father
For afternoon drinks, BBQ
And a swim in the pool.
Enjoying this Indian summer
And a day off with the kids.
The peace ends tomorrow
As back to work and the
Chaos of working with
Disorganised people will
No doubt drag me under again.
It was never my choice
To work this way.

John Davies 2018 ©

This wasn't my intention
To try and push for fame.
I make no gain.
I play no games.
I've been writing my
Whole life but wanted
To leave my legacy
Behind me for my children
To one day discover.
I have spent more money
On giving books away
Than actual sales. I do this
For no other reason than art.
Each book will bring me
A guaranteed one-star review.
What a life he must lead
Being obsessed with trying
To ruin everything I work hard
To create. I forgive ignorance
But find no love for those
Who only have hate in their hearts.

John Davies 2018 ©

The doves didn't cry
And the air was silent.
There was an impending
Mood outside that something
Amazing was about to happen.
Maybe a hurricane or the sky
Was just angry with the way
We treated its world down below.
We were greedy in most parts
And starving in others.
We killed each other and
Beautiful animals for profit.
Made ugly ornaments to hang
On cheap walls in pretentious
Offices. It was our way of showing
Wealth and power. I decided
One day I would write poetry
And release books. Of all the
People that got it, one person
Made it his business to try
And ruin mine. I laugh at his
One-star reviews and insults.
I used to feel sorry for him.
I must be a sad life being
That type of person after all.

John Davies 2018 ©

Looking up the night
Sky I see fireflies
Circling and illuminating
The path before me.
It wasn't my choice
To walk among the
Darkness but poor life
Choices and fate bound us
Together in a death grip
That would only expire
When I was no longer needed.
I turned around to look
For you but in the blink
Of an eye you were gone.

John Davies 2018 ©

Life is like a jigsaw
With many fragmentations
And pieces missing
In which we spend the
Best part of our lives
Trying to put back together.
We build our personality
Piece by piece until we
Are left with a picture
That only we are happy with.
It's a design that we will
Look at forever as it has
Become our mental image
Of what we eventually became.

John Davies 2018 ©

You lost me after your
First comment. I was no
Fucking side show for
Anyone. If you didn't want
To hang with the weird
Then you should never have
Put that kind of tag on
Yourself. Nobody is impressed
With a fraud. Continue to
Treat the world with contempt
And live your fictitious life.
I hope it makes you feel better
When at least one person
Likes your posts. We are easily
Removed from reality these
Days and we let social media
Become judge, jury and
Executioner playing out to
A tired audience who no longer
Clap at your performances.

John Davies 2018 ©

Sleep doesn't come easy
These days. Usually four
Hours on the sofa is all
I can muster up.
The mind became a
Landslide and the cogs
Of the machine had no
Off button. I wonder if it is
Possible to drive ourselves
Mad. I read a book on
Sleep deprivation and I
Am still not convinced.
I'll turn the TV back on
And drift away again.

John Davies 2018 ©

The cartoon waiter with his head
On a serving tray was always
A favourite when I was
A kid. I watch cartoons
These days and realise
How stupid they really are.
I moved over to Jason,
Freddy & Michael. The 1980's
Really knew how to create
A monster. Just like modern day
America with their idiot President
Donald Trump. As kids, monsters
Were a figment of our imagination.
Now we know that they
Come in many forms.

John Davies 2018 ©

I sit here at a loss.
I drink moonshine
And soda water
And the candles die
Like my enthusiasm
Towards my job and
Life right now.
Girls with stupid looking
Fake tits walk past me
And they expect
A hard on from
Their plastic creation.
We were never impressed
In the first place.
The lights go out
And somewhere a new
Life enters the world
With a scream.

John Davies 2018 ©

There was thunder
In your eyes
But yet I felt attracted
To the danger
That I knew would
Come with any
Association with someone
Like you. I was ageing
And getting tired of
The normal day to day
Life of being me.
I needed something
To kick start a revolution.
An awakening.
I asked questions
Of everyone, yet allowed
Myself to dodge the truth.

John Davies 2018 ©

Time runs out
For us daily
And we sit alone
Reciting old successes
When we are actually
Feeling defeated
And a little bit lost.
I drank alone in the dark
And the more I lost
My mind to the Devil
That controls me
I realized that there
Was still something left
To fight for. A snapshot
Of a life fallen to the gutter.
A glimpse of Phoenix's
Rising from the flames.
I felt liberated. I felt like
I still had a purpose here.

John Davies 2018 ©

Tonight
I decided
To retire
From writing.
I don't have
The time
Or passion
To find 5 seconds
To myself
These days.
This makes me
Feel selfish.
The general public
Loves pictures
After all.
Not poetry.

John Davies 2018 ©

Sitting in your pool
Drinking rhubarb gin
And digesting soul food.
We were singing along
To the soundtrack
Of Grease & The Bee Gees.
It felt like summer
And then it started to rain
Down on us all.

John Davies 2018 ©

For the smiles.
The laughter.
The tears.
The sadness.
The mood swings.
The kisses.
The hugs.
The dirty nappies.
The attitude.
The sleepless nights.
You are my children
And I will always
Love you unconditionally.

John Davies 2018 ©

Blank margin
Equals blank cheque.
Lack of production
Lack of organization.
Been accused of it all.
Too many politics bred
In this environment that
We find ourselves in right now.
Retain equilibrium.
Dance with the stars
And aim high. We are models
Of this modern world. We can fly.

John Davies 2018 ©

Dusty boots scrape across
The Nevada plains.
Dust devils whisper
The suggestion of
The end of our tired
Souls. The taste of sand
In our mouths and
Delirium drives us
Toward our peyote dreams.
As we swim with the mad
And the unknown. We look for
A way home, but have no direction.

John Davies 2018 ©

We sold out too many
Times while saying it
Would be for the very
Last time. Each time we
Looked at ourselves
In the mirror and knew
We were only cheating
Ourselves. We live a lie
Throughout our time
Here and it is our legacy
That defines whether
Our journey was a success
Or a failure. We get too
Weighed down by other
Peoples drama and make it
Our own only to see them
Free of their issues
While we are chained
And suffocating from them
Because we cared enough
To try to help. It left us
With nothing. We will just
Be a picture on the wall
Clouded in dust and packed
Away in a trash can one day.
Our lives irrelevant.
Easily erased. Easily forgotten.

John Davies 2018 ©

I was a fool for you
And eventually
You would be my
Downfall. I spent so
Much time worrying
About trying to make
You happy that I didn't
See the illness until
It became out of control
And too late to save
Myself. I was racing
Along life too fast
And not paying attention
To the dangers that were
All around me. I took people
For granted, I got bored
Easily of people who always
Gave their time up for me
On a whim. I became
High maintenance
And eventually
Everyone left.
They always do.
But as Stephen King
Would say,
Sometimes they come back!

John Davies 2018 ©

I watched the drunks
Fighting over a half
Empty bottle of malt
And picking at scabs
On their heads
While all around them
The world continued.
Oblivious to their meager
Existence. In one corner
We had the essence of America
Driving around in their
Muscle cars and flash suits
With their trophy Wives,
And 6 feet away the sewer
Rats read Allen Ginsberg
And rustled through garbage
Cans. Middle America amazes me.
They elected an idiot to be
Their President who wanted to
Build a wall to cut off Mexico?
Buy him a lot of Lego bricks
And make him build it himself.

John Davies 2018 ©

Head slumped and mind
Burning at 2pm in the
Afternoon. The smell of
Last night's sex and puke
In the rest rooms
And your feet are still
Stuck to the floor
Like you had glue pads
Fixed on. The usual
Bar flies sipping away
Their retirement funds
And looking at anyone
With suspicion with
Wet, red, glassy eyes.
Food arrives from a
Microwave and is lesser
Than a ready meal but
You eat it anyway.
Hotel California playing
In the background
And you realise that
This is the kind of place
Where you can disappear
Forever and never be found again.

John Davies 2018 ©

The body is a machine.
We feed it the fuel
Which can make it perform
Or destroy it.
We grow tired the older
We get and if we feed
Our bodies a constant
Flow of alcohol and
Fatty foods we will
Kill it and become extinct.
This makes me the
Ultimate hypocrite.
I needed to take better care
Of myself but didn't
Know how too.

John Davies 2018 ©

We all have our little trials
And successes throughout
Our lives and no matter how far
We fall, there is always
The realization that no
Matter how hard it seems,
There is always a silver lining.
We have air to breathe.
Food to eat. Water to nourish.
We are in a temporary struggle
That we always had the
Answers too and a way out.
We sat too close to the problem
While the solution was already
Within our very grasp all the time.

John Davies 2018 ©

She gave me a candle
That she said would never
Burn out. A light that would
Never dim or stop glowing.
A beacon into faraway worlds
And unknown pleasures
And mysterious endeavors.
She gave me a candle
That would never burn
My fingers to the touch.
She gave me joy, in fact
She gave me too much.
She gave me a candle
Straight away from the start.
But it wasn't a candle
In fact, it was her heart.

John Davies 2018 ©

We lose ourselves
Along the way
And find our interior
Compasses no longer
Correlate to our current
Juxtaposition. I read somewhere
In a cheap throw away paper
That we pass many people
With invisible faces who
At one stage in our lives
We either knew or threw away
When we were knee deep
In our developmental years.
Life's passengers who at our
Earliest convenience we threw
Directly off the bus
To continue our journey alone.

John Davies 2018 ©

It was really that simple.
I was tired
I was soulless
I had too much
Going on for your
Continuous demands
And eventually
Like everything
In life
I had to walk away
And call it quits.
It was the only way
I could stay sane
And look in that mirror
Again, before I pulled
That rope and rocked
That chair from under
My feet like my late brother
Did when his demons
Got the better of him.

John Davies 2018 ©

It was always going
To be a recipe for disaster.
You were a hell raiser
And as we drank the night
Away I knew the hour
Had passed out on us again.
We were staying in a hostel
Somewhere in the middle
Of nowhere and the locals
Became a little too friendly.
It appeared that they were
Hungry for some kind
Of action and we somehow
Had become the main attraction.
I went to order food but
Only found myself on the menu.
The exit out had become blocked
And as a sea of vampires
Descended on me, my final thoughts
Were dimmed by a blow
To the back of the head.
I woke up in a damp sweat.
It had been a dream after all.

John Davies 2018 ©

The taste of cheap wine
And the smell of cheap
Perfume were the aromas
In the air at this dive bar.
I told myself that this would be
The very last time I'd stop by
But was drawn by the allure
Of stalking the dangers
That sent my adrenaline
Over the edge. I sat in a suit.
An easy target to some.
Yet nobody approached.
Maybe I looked insane after all.

John Davies 2018 ©

We walk around
Damaged goods.
Life already taken
Its toll on us.
It's a day by day
Challenge to keep
This smile on our faces.
We have credit cards
And overdrawn accounts
And even then, we struggle
To keep our heads afloat
Each month. We live in
A HP world that drain what
Little we have left with
Interest. I don't know who
Is better off these days.
The homeless man staring
At me while eating his lunch
Or me racing to the train
Station with the weight
Of the world on my shoulders
And mouths to feed?

John Davies 2018 ©

It was meant to be
Easy at the beginning
Yet we swam against
The tide and the walls
Fell down around us.
You were always the one
Who was late to the party
And the very first to leave.
I wasn't offended. It just made
It easier to remove you
From my life before we
Got too close to each other.

John Davies 2018 ©

Death has a very
Strange relationship
With me and my family.
It took away my everything
Leaving me in the void
Looking into the darkness
And alone. But I don't fear
It's existence. How can I?
We are so well acquainted
That every time there
Is a knock on the door
I am already saying
Goodbye to what's left
Of my little family.

John Davies 2018 ©

We are all part of a bigger picture
We serve a higher purpose
And even though we don't
Realise it, we have already
Been programmed by
The system. We are addicted
To social media and reality
TV shows, we cheer the winner
At every opportunity
As our egos won't allow us
To be on the losing side.
We compete relentlessly
With one another no matter
What the personal cost is.
We have become almost
Primitive in our outlook and
Quest for goals that we miss
The most important thing
Around us. The ones we love
Always compete for our attention
But we are always too busy
To acknowledge them.
By our own affirmation
We've already made them extinct.

John Davies 2018 ©

Life is a jigsaw puzzle
And sometimes it takes
Us longer to finish
Than others. Never lose
Sight of the fact that
The end result will
Define us as people and
How we progress.
Be that star in the sky
Full of thunder & clouds.

John Davies 2018 ©

I sit on the late
Night train and my
Whole day has been
Lost. It's time I will
Never get back and
Time is all I am aware
Of these days as I
Get older and cherish each
Moment I spend with
You all. We encompass
Our thoughts and share
Memories and it makes
Life more tenable and
Happier to manage.
I work for a machine that
Chews me up daily
Yet I am forced to go
Back for more.

John Davies 2018 ©

There will always be haters.
They find their way
Into our lives uninvited
And smear their own
Brand of slime over
Everything we hold dear.
Our pictures, our poems
And our reputations.
Social media made it
Easy to be a target
For those who have nothing
Better to do with there
Own lives. Cyber bullying.
Poisonous keyboard cowards.
The secret is to grow
Another layer, a second armour
And to continue doing what
You love without being
Affected by the stupidity
Of it all.

John Davies 2018 ©

Fake accounts
Under fake names
To follow me on
Instagram and to
Continue to write
Rubbish about me
And re write the poems
I posted. I can deal with
Childish insults but when
People start dissecting
My work and start
Slandering me as a person
The line has well and truly
Been crossed. I will continue
To block these fake accounts
In the hope that one day
This person finally
Gets a life and grows up!
Obsessing about others
Is not a healthy thing to do?
It will slowly drive you insane
If it hasn't already.

John Davies 2018 ©

I waited until breakfast
Time had finished.
I was never a coffee
And croissant kind of guy
So, I fed the kids a combination
Of calories and put on
Their favourite movie
While I awaited the
Witching Hour. 12pm and
I made my way into
The kitchen and found
The elixir of the Gods.
As I poured from the bottle
I told myself it was alright
To be a narcissist
And what I was doing was
Normal. My diet needs some
Working on as the middle aged
Spread is turning into a tyre
And I'm bored of walking
Around work all day
Holding in my breath
So my shirt buttons don't
Pop off into the sunset.

John Davies 2018 ©

I felt the wind coming from
The ocean and the sway of
The palm trees
Told me summer
Was almost over.
We sat under the stars
Toasting marshmallows
And cooking steaks
While the smell of sea
Air and sand mixed
Into the aromas.
We knew moments
Like this were few and far
Between as we had moved
On from one another
And this was the
Inevitability of a dying
Friendship. Our time was
Almost at an end
And as we surveyed
Our surroundings one last time
You poured Jack Daniels
Neat and threw back
A shot. Faraway we heard
Familiar sounds stalking
The night. We knew the demons
Had finally come to claim
Our benevolent souls.

John Davies 2018 ©

Rodeo Drive
Beverly Hills
Wilshere Boulevard.
Walk of style.
Nude sculpture
"Torso"
Robert Graham.
Acclaimed sculpture.
The characteristics
Of the rich and famous.
Style council.
Heritage.
I'd take a flight
And buy a mansion
If only I had the money
To play roulette.

John Davies 2018 ©

We drove past
Laurel Canyon
And still sensed
A feeling of the 1960's.
The summer of love
And the ghost of
Jim Morrison still
Lingering everywhere.
This is a place where
Time stood still and the
Romance never left.
A Mustang passed down
Love Street and I heard
The Devil of Rock
Singing Light my Fire.
All of the history lost
To us. This was once a
Peaceful place to be.

John Davies 2018 ©

We flick through our
Smart phones and
Glide through the
Thousands of options
Afforded to us at the
Risk of ignoring the
Whole world & everyone
Around us. We have become
Techno Zombies in a time
Of chaos and fake news.
You walk past disused
Telephones boxes.
Dinosaurs of another age.
We once used to scroll through
Large phone books and wait
To be connected by an
Operator. Yes, it took longer
But people were more connected
To one another unlike today.
Technology went forward
Yet we somehow went
Backwards as people.

John Davies 2018 ©

Be someone's
Destination
Not just part
Of their journey.
Remove the emotional
Clutter that others
Leave behind
For you to clean up
After and drive
Into the night
With a clear direction
Of where you're going.
As through life
It is easy to get lost
Within the traffic.

John Davies 2018 ©

There was a time
Once when I cared
About adverse
Publicity. Then I realized
That no matter how
Hard you try to deflect
The silent blows
Aimed your way
There is always a jealous
Mind hiding in the
Shadows waiting to
Create its own drama.
They want the response
From hurting you as the
World has already
Forgotten them and they
Have nothing left to
Cling onto to appease
Their sorry little lives.

John Davies 2018 ©

I looked into your
Dead eyes and I
Understood perfectly.
You were never going
To be mine and no
Matter how hard I tried
You would be a smear
On my mind forever.
You instantly made
For the door before it
Had even shut close.
The linger of your perfume
Was all that you gave to me
To serve as a lasting
Memory of our brief time together.

John Davies 2018 ©

He walked into his
Local pub and gambled
His money in the
Fruit machine. He spent
10 hours a day as a
Call centre assistant and
Spent hours alone in his
Seedy little flat watching
Porn and drinking cheap
Supermarket beer
Deciding to troll people
Because the talent he thought
That he had was never
Really there. It made him mad
That his best friend stole
His girlfriend for a bag of chips
And a gin and tonic
One night down the Railway Inn.
He looks at the dregs of
His Guinness glass and decides to play
On the one-armed bandits
One last time in the hope
That he'd win a fiver and tomorrow
Would be a better day.

John Davies 2018 ©

The day is done
For now. I sit alone
In a strange town
Awaiting a ghost train
With a cold beer and
A banana skin left
On the chair beside me.
Four feet away is a litter bin.
Was it too much trouble?
Am off to say goodbye
To a few old friends
I used to work with.
Still suited. No time to change.
My eyes keep drifting
To that banana skin. The sun
Is having a rare visit
But my mind keeps
Thinking about bananas
And Andy Warhol's
Painting of them.

John Davies 2018 ©

The rich and poor
Have one thing in common.
Every human being
Views the world with
The same eyes and sees
The same sunset each
And every evening.
Some sleep under the stars
And some sleep in
Well-made beds. I rested
My head on the bosom
Of the world and felt
Her heartbeat go straight
Through me.

John Davies 2018 ©

The solitude at night
On a lonely train.
That long journey home
To where you really
Feel safe. That place where
Your soul belongs and
That will always be
Your comfort zone.
It is almost midnight
And me and a handful
Of lonely hearts are just
Trying to find our way home again.

John Davies 2018 ©

I am made up from
Layers of everyone
I have ever met or had
Friendships or relationships with.
I have absorbed
A piece of every one
Of you and whether
It's a good thing or a
Bad trait I am stuck
Like this forever now.
Every person left there
Own indelible mark
On me whether I like
It or not. What I am now
Is what I've finally became.

John Davies 2018 ©

I worry about the nervous
Northern lad with not
Too many friends.
He sits behind a keyboard
Playing cool but then
Has to walk down the
Beautiful streets of Barnsley
To grab a fried Mars bar
And Iron Brew. I wonder if
He was bullied as a child.
Abused or pinned down
In the school play yard
And pissed on and buggered
By the local bully.
You see what you did?
You see what you did!!
You poked a bear
And this bear bites!!

John Davies 2018 ©

Wonky Bollins had a voucher
At the local corner shop.
He had a Jack Russell dog.
It shits on his bed daily.
He fell out of bed daily.
He fell out of bed and tripped
Over empty Special Brew cans.
He crawled to the toilet
And sat there with his
Head in his hands while a
Nothing band he made
Homemade homage videos
For and posted on YouTube
Tried to become famous again.
Even though they didn't make it
First time around in the 90's.
The lead singer tried his hardest
To sound like Liam Gallagher.
He grew a beard to hide
His ugliness and became bitter
As he was never going
To amount to much.
I sent him an email about
Job opportunities that
Would have set him back
On track. Mc'Ronalds wanted
A fry cook. He failed the interview.

John Davies 2018 ©

King of the Sunset Strip Volume Three: The Poetry Collection.

Wonky Bollins walked into
His local Cost Cutter shop
Up north like. He was hanging
After listening to music
He hated, but thought it
Made him look cool by name
Checking them. Even though
They never made the big time.
He made fake accounts
And writ some hilarious
Shin digs at me. I laughed
Then blocked the prick.
Am guessing right now
He is watching TV re runs of
Jim'll Fix It while listening
To Gary Glitter's greatest hits
Collection. He has issues.
Stella in one hand
Thumb up his rectum searching
For the male G Spot.
Mate, I'd hate to be you right now.

John Davies 2018 ©

How many times
I pick up this pen
And wear the same
Suit while the world
Sleeps and I am still
Waiting at another
Train platform. It gets dark
These days and for every
Delayed departure
I lose another hour in bed.
Tomorrow's alarm call
Will mock me and leave
Me gasping for air as I
Soon realise that it was
All a dream and I'd
Never actually slept at all.

John Davies 2018 ©

Sometimes we feel old.
We feel tired.
We look at our bodies
And wonder if we have
Enough time left to
Make a dying machine
Young and ripped again.
We try to decrease
The ageing process through
A Porsche and a midlife
Crisis instead of planning
Ahead and looking
Forward to our Indian summers
And re-education as elders
Or grandparents. I was a reluctant
Older Father at first. I regret that now.
I feel selfish as I've given life
To two young, beautiful boys
Who needed me in my prime
Where I had many more years
Left on the clock to spend with them.

John Davies 2018 ©

I tickled the inside
Of your thigh and
For a while I saw
A flicker of a smile
Make a short appearance
On your face.
It was like an Angel
Looking down on me
And for that moment
Alone, I felt like I could
Rule the world.
You made me immortal
And I got drunk
On that power over you.

John Davies 2018 ©

I have the motion
And the motive.
I'll leave the rest
In your hands.
They felt warm to me.
I stand in the dark
Engulfed in its cold caress.
I strangely feel at home
Like this. No one can see
My face and the world
Is finally quiet except
For the noisy taxi drivers
Smoking cheap cigarettes
And speaking in a strange
Tongue of which I cannot
Decipher. I pullup an App
On my phone and it tells me
My Uber ride is almost here.
I watch the sea of taxi's
Sat there like iron chariots
And smile as I've just saved
A fortune and my return
Home is imminent.

John Davies 2018 ©

Sip a cold beer
At the end of a long day.
Throw caution
To the wind and feel
That release of stress
As the chill hits your tongue.
A lady tripped over her
Shoe lace on the way to the
Train station as she was
Paying way too much attention
To the phone in her hand.
She scuffed her knees
And the blood made her
Look like she'd been doing
Something else instead.
Some people laughed.
I felt genuinely embarrassed
For her. I walked over to ask
If she was alright, but she told
Me to go away. Made me wish
That the next time she fell over
She fell harder and learnt
Some basic manners and
Decorum in the very near future.

John Davies 2018 ©

Snakeskin eyes
Lizard skin
The demon searches
Way within
The sorcery used
To pull me in
It overwhelms
That trance I'm in
I fight the power
I feed its greed
Had he become
My friend indeed
As I lay down
For my last breath
I know you will not
Love me any less.

John Davies 2018 ©

The voices all compete
With one another.
Each one fighting
To be heard. The fake
Laughs and elaborate
Bullshit stories aimed
To stand above the crowd.
To seek the attention.
I hate these voices.
I wish they would leave.

John Davies 2018 ©

There will always be haters.
They find their way
Into our lives
Uninvited and smear
Their own brand of slime
Over everything we hold dear.
Our pictures, our poems
And our reputations.
Social media has made it
Easy to be a target for those
Who has nothing better
To do with their own lives.
Cyber bullying. Poisonous
Keyboard cowards.
The secret is to grow another
Layer. A second armour
And to continue doing what
You love without being affected
By the stupidity of it all.

John Davies 2018 ©

The curator of the tale
Sick from his madness
Pokes at the embers
Of his forest fire.
He listens to what
The night is telling him
And sighs. He gulps down
A greedy mouthful
Of cognac and wishes
That times were simpler
Once more. A survivor of
The urban wars. Now a shadow
Never seen. Never spoken about.
He found comfort in his solitude
However, his ego needed more.

John Davies 2018 ©

Sometimes we feel old. We feel tired.
We looked at our bodies
And wonder if we have
Enough time left to make
A dying machine young and ripped again.
We try to decrease
The ageing process through
A Porsche and a midlife
Crisis instead of planning
Ahead and looking forward
To our Indian summers
And re-education as elders
Or Grandparents.

John Davies 2018 ©

Every story has
A hero.
Every story has
A villain.
Don't be confused
With either one
Of this cast.
People change
Unfortunately
Way too easily
And you are often
Left with a bloody nose
And a tear running
Down your cheek.
This is the legacy
Of their love
That they have
Left you to deal with.

John Davies 2018 ©

Haiku. Sentimental.
A prose and a muse.
You were made in the
Shape of an Angel.
Watching me always.
In my eyes I saw you.
In each beat of my heart
I fell in love with you
All over again.
I felt at one again.
I felt complete.

John Davies 2018 ©

I was the last follower
Here on Earth
You wanted
And you would
Take me at any cost.
Your Human trophy
To take back to Hell
As competition
For the Devil.
I saw us as equals
But you viewed me
Far superior to the
King of the dark side.
I felt flattered having
Such big hooves to feel.

John Davies 2018 ©

The end game
Has no winners.
We live in a dying age
With no respect
For the time
And the hours
We put in during
Our time here.
We depart already
Forgotten.
We should have
Meant more to others
As they did to us.

John Davies 2018 ©

Don't fight with me
You are playing with
The Devil's favourite Demon.
And I have a zero
Tolerance approach
To other people's drama.
You want action?
Get off your asses and
Make a statement.
Take your eyes away from
Your mobile phones and
Duck face pictures.
Be relevant and live every
Moment. Ever thought about
How many people saw you
As a cunt posing with
A phone in front of your face?
If that is cool in 2018
It makes me glad that I still
Live the values of the 1980's.
I did selfies once.
Finally got bored
Of my own face!

John Davies 2018 ©

It was hard being
The object of your desire.
We savour the compliments
And the attention until
It finally gets to the point
Where it is apparent that
The attention is more
About control than ownership.
Tired of the constant arguments
About the 30 seconds I was
Out of your eyesight for a call
Of nature. I was balls deep
Inside a porcelain bowl
Spilling my guts out literally
To a ghost audience.
I zipped up my pants
And walked straight past you
And out the front door.
I'd send someone over
Tomorrow for my luggage.
Buy yourself a puppy.
Humans don't need to be
Owned and it was apparent
That you needed me far more
Than I needed the strangulation
That life with you had
In store for me.

John Davies 2018 ©

Love me for who
I am, for as long as
The time we have together
Is short, we can make
Every moment count.
Love me for my weaknesses.
My addictions. My mistakes.
(and I make many). Love me
If only for the fact that
No matter how complex
I am, I truly do love you back.
Events throughout my life
Have made it almost
Impossible for me to show
Real emotion at the turn
Of a tap. Love me for who
I am. If only because one day
I'll no longer be here
To love or be hated anymore.

John Davies 2018 ©

The evolution of our
Inner sanctum
Represents the corners
Of the world we currently inhabit.
It is all too easy
To find yourself in a dark place.
The secret is how you learn
To remove yourself
From that darkness & seek the light.
Without that, the chances are
This losing streak will never end!

John Davies 2018 ©

Filthy McNasty's.
Sunset Strip.
Black and white
Polaroid on the internet.
I wasn't alive
Around that time
But I am guessing
It was the best
Dive bar in town.
All the crack whores
Sucked dick through
Two front teeth
While still high from
Their visit to the crack
Meth lab. They finally
Graduated to the death drug.
Tired expressions on their
Sunken faces. Skin, bone
And lipstick. Dead eyes.
They called this the end
Of the summer of love
And all the freaks were
Dying out quickly!
Edging their way back
Into the gutter.
They'd be no survivors
In this town.

John Davies 2018 ©

We leave every person
And our legacy behind.
We become a gravestone.
Or a full Urn that
Gathers dust on a fire place.
I fear about the life
I will leave behind
As my children are young
And the world hasn't
Stuck its claw into
Their beautiful skin yet.
As a Father it makes me sad.
The knowledge of one day
Leaving these two beauties
Behind and never seeing
Their pretty faces again
Absolutely breaks my heart.
But I know it's inevitable
We all eventually tap out.
The sadness is always there.
Some of us just refuse
To acknowledge it.

John Davies 2018 ©

The mystery remained
In her eyes
And all they had seen
In a turbulent life
Now just a faded
Memory. Hers to keep
As she moved onto
Pastures new.
The thing about some
People is that they
Can easily remove you
And not feel a single
Thing as they walk away.
Not even your final goodbye.

John Davies 2018 ©

Drinking pink Lanson
Champagne and chopping
Beef tomatoes and basil
In the kitchen under
Candle light with Eminem
Shouting at me about
The way I am is about
As perfect as my night
Can get right now. I'm a writer.
I publish books. Get drunk.
Enjoy dive bar fist fights.
I'll never be Charles Bukowski
As he was a big drinker
And a big thinker and he
Fucked whores and let them
Stay on the couch. I admire
The blues in his soul
And decades after his death
I still see him as a teacher.

John Davies 2018 ©

Everything said and done
I consider myself lucky.
I give more than I receive
And always look for the
Very best in every one.
I value every friendship
And hold love for those
Old and new in my life
That have always been there.
And to the others who have
Just arrived, welcome aboard
And enjoy the ride.

John Davies 2018 ©

Was it the thought
Of San Francisco
Or Texas that made
My mind go into overdrive.
I wanted the steak
But the pussy in Texas
Made the dessert seem
Much more appealing.
Alcatraz was an epic visit
But I loved running with
The bull and hanging with
The pretty girls with
Hooters T-shirts on.

John Davies 2018 ©

From the very depths
Of your soul, you gave me
The biggest challenge
Of my life. I was somehow
Meant to collaborate with
The words and darkness
Those three pages by you
Suggested and already I felt
The weight of your pain.
I was somehow meant to
Compliment the story you told
Knowing that this was the
Very beginning of our journey
Into the unknown together.
The abyss is deep enough
Before you stare down into
Other people's version of Hell.
But I'm up for the challenge.
Let's write a masterpiece.

John Davies 2018 ©

The first fist to the face
Was a defeating blow
But that was somehow
Relaxing as I knew
Of the pain yet still
To come as you exercised
That power over me.
Sure, I could learn to fight
But the past had taught me
That no matter how hard
I tried, you'd always
Have the upper hand.
The hand of destiny
Was dealt to me from
A stack of dirty playing cards
Stained by years of
Misuse and deception.
But I was the one always
In the wrong with a bruised heart
And broken ribs.
A modern day take on love
Came in the shape
Of a clenched fist
And the promised that
You'd never do it again.

John Davies 2018 ©

We are all paradox's
Dispose of those around
You that bring darkness
Into your lives.
Death soldiers on
Over the horizon
And the vulnerable
Stand still like targets
Awaiting their fate
And a warm, milky
Execution. We can run
With the crowd or
Stand and fight
For another day here.

John Davies 2018 ©

She sat beside me at
The train station.
It was 6am, maybe a few
Minutes past. Scuffed knees,
Red rimmed eyes and
Running mascara. My first
Guess was tears. There was
A smell of fear and sex
About her. I got a feeling
That it wasn't consensual.
I offered her my jacket
And she viewed me with
Suspicion. It broke my heart
To think that anyone
Thought they had the
Right to break
Something so fragile.

John Davies 2018 ©

I don't want to drag my heels
And stumble through life.
I want to be that shooting star.
You know, the one that is seen
One-night flying across the sky
And then the next minute is gone.
But in the short time it was there
I your presence, it illuminated
Everything around it and gave
Everyone something to remember
It by. That's how I see myself.

John Davies 2018 ©

Never be defeated
Or lose the energy
That makes you who
You are. There's a queue
A mile long ready to
Knock you from your podium.
Forever jealous of your
Success. See past the dark
Clouds they hang over your head.
Put your umbrella up
And continue to walk through
The storm that life
Has in store for you.
Take on each day
With a smile.

John Davies 2018 ©

King of the Sunset Strip Volume Three: The Poetry Collection.

Part Two: Rodeo Drive - Lexicon Devil.

"Each of us experiment with the dark. Some find solace in the knowledge that we are not alone, while others take refuge in the silence & solitude of their own homes. We were all born different, and enjoy different things. Never try to be anyone else but yourself. It's a losing game".

John Davies 2018 ©.

She had the taste of
A low class whore
In her mouth and
Wondered why you evaded
Her kiss. She stumbled
On broken heels and looked
Like the street car pro
From that car scene in
The Last Exit to Brooklyn.
The only thing that sparkled
About her were those few
Gold coins that spilled
Out of her purse and onto
The sidewalk as she fumbled
For your zipper and you
Pushed her away.
Laughing into the night
You pulled out a cigar
And hailed a ride home.

John Davies 2018 ©

The sound of glass
Shattering against the wall
And the scream awakens
You in the night.
Underneath your bedroom
Window is a dark alleyway
Where all the tough guys
Hang out and peddle there
Ladies deep into the early
Hours of the morning.
You peek through a crack
In your curtains and see a face
Staring up at you in anger.
Were you there all along?
A crash of a downstairs door
And thunderous footsteps
Gaining speed. Suddenly there's
A knock on your door and you
Know the devil has arrived
For your soul.

John Davies 2018 ©

You hung around darkened
Clubs like The Borderline
& the 100 Club desperate
To see somebody relevant
But those cats had left the
Building and the smell
Of sweat and beer were
All that lingered in their wake.
The bands had packed their
Guitars up and only the jukebox
Was left playing the dulcet
Tunes of legends like Iggy Pop,
The Dead Kennedys & Spizz Energi.
You took to the bar and ordered
Another shot of whisky
Before the doors closed for the
Night knowing for that moment
You were alone with the voices
Of Gods booming in your ears.
Nothing could take that feeling
Of sheer bliss away from you.
And for that short time –
You felt Immortal.

John Davies 2018 ©

Just because she
Gave you head
Doesn't mean she
Loves you?
Stop vanity
Getting in the way
Of pleasure.
It's a vitamin shot
For her & an ego
Boost for you.

John Davies 2018 ©

My next door neighbour
Stood in the rain
Watering her giant
Sunflower. I said to her
"Hey De-De, the rain will
Take care of that for you?"
She stopped what she was doing
And looked at me like I was crazy
And replied "I know but tonight
Could be my last night on earth
And if I don't water it tonight
It might die?". With that she
Smiled and said goodnight.
I never saw her again.

John Davies 2018 ©

I thought about the Barnsley
Gimp and his alter ego
Tonight and it made me chuckle.
If you're going to call out
A better writer / poet
Then bring out the big guns
And don't embarrass your dumb northern ass.
It's not a competition?
If so, you'd never be invited!
I get that working for £3.42
Per hour cleaning toilets in the
Local community centre has
No perks. I get that man!
I get that trying to befriend failed
1990's "Indie" stars like The Voss
And doing shitty videos on
YouTube would be your sacrifice
To the ego. But where did it get you?
Oh, it got you me. And trolling me?
How's that working out for you?
Bad I'm guessing as you don't have
The vocabulary or talent to touch me.
Grab a white towel. Wave it and throw
It towards anyone who cares.

John Davies 2018 ©

Eclipsed by that sudden
Movement in your eyes
I fell in love
All over again and
The heat of the fire
Inside me consumed
Me to the core.
I realized then
On that day
I could never live
Without you for even
One second.

John Davies 2018 ©

Halloween is dawning.
A time when most of
Our inner demons
Come out to play
Which is strange as
The real monsters walk
Around daily without masks
And costumes, just disguised
As normal people living
Normal lives, wearing suits
And dresses and convincing
Us otherwise.

John Davies 2018 ©

I stand in the shadow
Of greatness and never
Once did it faze me.
I look to my left and
The Adonis figure of
A modern-day God
Smiles in my direction.
Apparently the two of us
Are friends and have always
Known of one another.
I had a watcher in
My dreams and always
Woke up none the wiser.
It was time to take a
Seat and parlay late
Into the night. No words escaped
My mouth. For once
I was speechless.

John Davies 2018 ©

You banished me away
Into the cheap seats
Never to return
Never to speak again
Because my words
Offended you.
The truth hurt
Like a kick in the teeth.
I drank my lager
Threw away the last
Of my fries
And tipped the waiter
As I stepped into the night.
It was a cool evening
And I had finally lost
My last piece of baggage.

John Davies 2018 ©

We are instantly
Forgotten
And instantly
Removed
From that last
Person to throw
You in the garbage bin.
Our hearts will heal
Eventually as that's
What we do
Once we've been thrown
Away again.
We carry on
As they move on.
Disposable humans.

John Davies 2018 ©

The scent lingers.
All of those usual
Things that reminded me
Of you. Nothing left but
The constant longing
Of wanting to see
You again, but the honest
Realization that you will
Never return cuts
Like a sharp knife
To the insides. I didn't get
To know you as well as
I wanted to. We had so much
More to do together.
Dreams that were ripped apart.
To my brothers I will always
Hold you deep inside my heart.

John Davies 2018 ©

I look at your
Photographs
And feel only
One thing.
Jealous.
Jealous that
I am not in them
With you
And never will be.

John Davies 2018 ©

Time is a
Commodity
We no
Longer treat
As a luxury
The older
We get.
It gets shorter
Each day and
Like the falling
Leaves, it drifts
Past us into
The still of the
Night never to be
Seen again.
A distant memory
Of what we
Once were.

John Davies 2018 ©

Love casts no shadow
Over me anymore.
Learn to focus on what is
Absolutely your priorities
In life and ensure that
You never lose touch
Of exactly why that is
So important to you.
We all bleed differently.
Some things hurt us more
Than others but equally
A kill shot is always
Just a second away.
Just don't get caught
In the crossfire.

John Davies 2018 ©

The velveteen feel
Of her thigh slicing through
The palms of your hand
As it continued its journey
Towards male heaven.
There is no filter
When it comes to this
Kind of thing. Exposure and poise.
The magic is in every single
One of us if only we choose
To explore one another.
There is lust around every corner
And we are a fool
To its every move.

John Davies 2018 ©

We abuse our bodies
On a daily basis.
Feed it the wrong fuel
Because of our
Addictions. We know we
Are slowly killing it
And ageing it, however
We are completely
Ignorant as we are
Addicted to a poison
That has a hold on us and
Is never willing to let
Us out of its grip.
We count the days
As days soon end.

John Davies 2018 ©

She drove a Dodge Charger
And lived her life
Like a Duke in Hazzard Town.
Wore a flannel shirt
With boobs greeting you
With a Hooters smile.
Hillbilly boots up to her knees.
She smelled of hay and country
And sounded like the ghost
Of Johnny Cash, but was
The most beautiful girl
In the world and I wanted
To marry her. Said she made
A wicked piece of apple pie.
I just wanted to taste
Her for myself.

John Davies 2018 ©

Your beauty stole
My view and I was forever
At odds with myself.
You led a separate life
And distilled in my brain
Was a wanting that
Would never end. It would
Eventually consume me
As I watched you fade
Deeper into the distance.
The lost highway beckoned you
And you were powerless
To the attraction it gave you.

John Davies 2018 ©

The wine ends and you
End up looking at the mixers.
This was a bad day
And you deserved a hell
Of a lot more than life
Gave you today.
Your plate is full from the
Corporate bullshit and
Cost cutting lies. You watch
The very best members
Of your team leave because
Of these cut backs and wonder
How much longer you can
Withstand the insanity
Before moving on yourself.
A board of directors thought
That their decisions over
Fillet steak and champagne
Would've had a much better
Response than this?

John Davies 2018 ©

I was watching the black girls
Queuing in the same line
As the white girls.
What a difference in culture
And class. Chicken ordered
With a smile versus salads
And duck faces pouting into an iPhone.
Watching them eat was a
Masterclass. Some picked
Daintily at their pieces
Of lettuce while others
Tore chunks out of their
Chicken thighs and cheesy chips.
As both groups left
I knew straight away who were
The most attractive
And the ones I'd want to
Hang with if I was a woman,
Or date if I was 20 years younger.
It's a great job I wasn't alive
In the prohibition days.
I'd be hanging from a tree
Right now for my views.

John Davies 2018 ©

The three of us walked
Hand in hand and for that
One small moment
I felt the magic.
The connection between
A father and his two young boys.
I then felt the sadness
As they eventually
Walked off ahead together
Holding hands and laughing.
I knew this was how it
Will one day be.
Just the two of them
And no longer me.
But I am failing them
And slowly tearing us away
From each other as I am
Selfish and the addiction
Will one day kill me.

John Davies 2018 ©

The impending doom
Of the ugly society
Skipping the pill and making
Babies they cannot afford.
Drunk sex. It's a blast that
The tax payer gets to go
Home to their own kids
And spend the night worrying
About the bills while the
Jobless idiots of today's society
Stay in bed having ugly person
Sex and creating more mutants.
I sometimes wonder of there
Is a defect in human DNA
Somewhere along the wank banks
Or like magnets, the pond feeders
Finally find each other.
The working class are the catch.
We pop up every time
To swallow the worm!

John Davies 2018 ©

King of the Sunset Strip Volume Three: The Poetry Collection.

The older I get
The more comfortable
I am with being alone.
We end up in a wooden box
Or incinerator regardless.
Yet essentially alone.
I spend my days without
Rest or respite. My lunch
Breaks only happen in my
Four hour broken sleeps.
Just the pull of my two boys
That recharge me. Fulfill me.
This should be easier
Yet the bad planning skills
Of a plonker has gifted me pain
While he can go home early again
After a day of staring at a screen
He cannot operate and adding
Nothing to a team that is
Desperately crying out for
More guidance and support.
Just realized I became the
Manager of this whole shit storm
Tonight and the water is high
Under my chin and inviting me
To drink her like a medicine.

John Davies 2018 ©

I walk my streets
As the wind beats down
On me. Leaving the night
Behind, it is Autumn's way
Of shedding its summer skin
And leaving the dust in
Its rear-view mirror.
It is pumpkin season.
Soon will be the glow of
Christmas lights and the smell
Of cinnamon and mulled wine.
I will be ready.

John Davies 2018 ©

When I grew up
We wined and dined
Our potential suitors.
These days it is
All about young boys
Pounding their meat
Into the pink valley
And then leaving
With a grin and a shrug.
Manners and class seem
To have died a long time ago.

John Davies 2018 ©

She sat under the pine tree.
The first signs of Autumn
Appearing. The leaves turning
A beautiful bronze and red hue.
Pine cones fallen by her feet
And sprigs of holly in her hair.
She looked like a china doll.
Delicate to the touch.
You walked past her
And she smiled. She sparkled
Like diamonds but her eyes
Looked like a dark lake.
A mystery you would never
Get the chance to uncover.
You turned around but she
Had disappeared. Was she the
Ghost of your imagination
Or your Guardian Angel?

John Davies 2018 ©

Ever get the feeling that
No matter how hard you try
It is never enough
For some people and that
The more you do,
The more that is expected
Of you. Drained from the
Rigmarole and the hand
Life dealt you,
You look for other avenues.
Follow different routes
Until you become inexplicably
Lost in the turmoil
Of it all and getting out
Alive is the hardest thing
That you will ever do.

John Davies 2018 ©

Don't ever stop doing the stupid shit
That defines you. You cannot look back
On an embarrassing moment
When you are no longer here.
The embarrassment lasts for seconds,
Not a lifetime. A lifetime lasts
For as long as it needs. The learnings,
The teachings, successes, failures,
Relationships, everything turns to dust
In the end. Don't waste time being
Angry, mad or upset at others, especially
Loved ones, as you never know if it will be
The last time you ever see them again.

John Davies 2018 ©

My blood turns cold
As I see you standing
In the distance. The fog makes
The scene all the more sinister
And I can see you staring
At me through dead eyes.
I have evaded you for the
Best part of my life but you
Are getting closer to your goal
And even harder to hide from.
I will one day fall at the wayside.
Defeated and I know you will
Be there on a black horse
Ready to send me back to Hell.
A place I feel comfortable with
But reluctant to return to.
I still have work to do here.
All I'm asking for is a little more time.

John Davies 2018 ©

You stood me up on a
Pedestal and told me
I was the only one.
I fell for the cheap talk
Sat in the cheap seats
Believing this was all part
Of some masterplan.
But I was viewing the world
With rose coloured glasses.
Little did I know I was one
Of many who thought they
Meant something to you,
And that big things were
Coming my way. I saw the lie.
Eventually. Was it too late?
I had to find a way out of here
Before I fell into disrepair
Like all the other broken toys
You left lying around
With no intention of fixing.

John Davies 2018 ©

Acknowledgements:

Finishing the last ever King of the Sunset Strip book has been a long journey for me, as it puts to rest my favourite series of books. I want to thank everyone who has read any of my poems on Instagram, or purchased any of them (the very few of you that have, that is, even to my constant troll, I thank him, you see, he has inspired some of my better work, so thank you).

My next book Confessions of a Bar Fly is almost finished, and will be available December 2018.

There is a list of names a mile long, but you all know who you are. I hope you enjoy this book, and look forward to the reviews and feedback.

Much love as always...

John Davies.
22/10/2018.

King of the Sunset Strip Volume Three: The Poetry Collection.

Printed in Great Britain
by Amazon